THE
Archive Photographs
SERIES
AROUND
SIDMOUTH

Sidmouth Cricket Club vs W.T. Cook's XI, 16 and 17 September 1926. Included in the strong side Mr Cook brought to the Fortfield Ground were J.B. 'Jack' (later Sir) Hobbs, arguably England's greatest batsman, Frank Woolley, the great Kent and England all-rounder, and L.C.H. 'Lionel' Palairet of Somerset and England. Sidmouth Cricket Club, formed in 1823, is one of the oldest in Devon, and few clubs can claim to have such ideal views as backgrounds for their games as that at Fortfield, with the handsome Regency Fortfield Terrace (built between 1790 and 1794) on one side, the town and St Giles and St Nicholas's Church peeping above the roofs on another, and the sweep of the Channel on a third. Despite the fairly recent introduction of league cricket into Devon, Sidmouth is still one of the favourite destinations of touring teams and in August alone the club stages around twenty midweek games. Teams above, back row, left to right: F.R. Powell, T.G. Grinter, N.S.M. Atkinson, A.S. Ling, E.J. Mercy (treasurer), Capt. A.B.D. Moore (assistant secretary). Second row: H. Tate, J. Moore, A.W.R. Matthews, L.P. Hedges, I. Sorenson, E.P. Mills, Capt. E. Buller, D.D. Holman, H.F. Piper, W. Parry, S. Falding. Third row: J.J. Bridges, A. Kempton, L.C.H. Palairet, W.T. Cook, F.H. Carroll, J.B. Hobbs, E.A. Fulcher, F.E. Woolley. Front: W.T. Quaife, L. Todd, A.G. Skinner.

THE
Archive Photographs
SERIES

AROUND
SIDMOUTH

Compiled by
Les Berry and Gerald Gosling

CHALFORD

First published 1994
Copyright © Gerald Gosling and Les Berry, 1994

The Chalford Publishing Company Limited
St Mary's Mill, Chalford, Stroud
Gloucestershire GL6 8NX

ISBN 0 7524 0137 8

Typesetting and origination by
The Chalford Publishing Company Ltd
Printed in Great Britain by
Redwood Books, Trowbridge

For our wives, Joyce and Violet

The beach at Sidmouth around 1905 with Sidmouth's lifeboat, the *Willam and Francis*, in the foreground.

Contents

Introduction   7

1.   Sidmouth – the Place   9

2.   Sidmouth – the People   33

3.   At Work...   51

4.   ... and Play   61

5.   Sidford and Sidbury   73

6.   Branscombe   101

7.   Newton Poppleford   117

Acknowledgements   128

Potbury's showrooms, High Street, Sidmouth, at the turn of the century. Sidmouth's oldest business, the auctioneer and furnishing firm, was started in 1849 by Charles Farrant and traded under its Farrant name until at least the end of the century, when it became Potbury & Sons. Charles Farrant, who died in 1861, was succeeded by Mrs Ann Farrant. Following the death of Mrs Ethel Potbury in the early 1970s, the business has been owned by the Lee family. If England is a nation of shopkeepers, the Farrants certainly appear to have been a family of them. In 1838, besides John Farrant & Son who were auctioneers, the following businesses could be found in the town: Richard Farrant (grocer), John Farrant (agent for the Globe Insurance Office), C. Farrant (agent for the Royal Exchange Insurance Office), another John Farrant (ironmonger and tinman), Richard Farrant (Wine & Spirit Merchant) and C. Farrant (straw-bonnet manufacturer).

Just a line from Sidmouth.

Introduction

Theodore H. Mogridge, in his *Descriptive Sketch of Sidmouth* in 1836, said he 'cheerfully presents...his little book to the inhabitants of Sidmouth...' I hope Les Berry and Gerald Gosling cheerfully present this book because it certainly cheered me to look through it and enjoy the changing story of one of England's loveliest seaside towns.

Sidmouth has it all: East Devon at its unsurpassable best as a backdrop, frowning hills to keep winter's chill winds away, a town packed with lovely old buildings, a seafront to savour and, over all, an air of genteel nineteenth-century respectability that the modern tourist trade will never be able to destroy.

It would be hard to know where to begin in Sidmouth. St Giles and St Nicholas's church is probably too new to interest the school who can only see beauty in a church if it is old, but it has much to commend it, not least the attractive West Window, which was a gift from Queen Victoria in memory of her father, Edward Duke of Kent, who came to Sidmouth with his family on Christmas Eve 1819 to escape his many creditors. St Giles and St Nicholas's was practically rebuilt in the 1850s, and today only the tower and part of the nave of the old building remains. But it was a handsome enough building when the infant Victoria arrived.

And it was a handsome enough town as well, many of the buildings so admired today having just been built, following the discovery of Sidmouth 'by the better classes' during the Napoleonic Wars, when the Continent was barred to them for their pleasure.

Sidmouth has continued to give pleasure – and not just to the 'better classes' – and long may it continue to do so.

Les and Gerald are to be commended on this excellent book showing us so much of our distant and not so distant past. I am particularly pleased that they have included Sidford among the surrounding villages, that village and its bigger neighbour having been together far too long not to be joined here as well.

Fred Bennett
Sidford 1995

The Grand Cinema shortly before its destruction by fire in the 1950s. Sidmouth's first films were shown in 1911 in the Manor Hall, and later in the Drill Hall. The Grand was opened in 1929 but, sadly, no longer used as a cinema after the fire. Today a restaurant occupies the site.

One
Sidmouth
The Place

Looking into Church Street from the Market Place, Sidmouth, c.1938.

St Giles and St Nicholas's church and Church Street, Sidmouth, c.1880. The church was almost entirely rebuilt in 1859, with only the tower and part of the nave remaining from the previous building. Norman remains were found during the rebuilding and were incorporated into the present building. The fine West Window was a gift of Queen Victoria to the memory of her father, the Duke of Kent.

Church Street, Sidmouth, c.1914. Miss Emily Skinner, sister to Arthur Skinner, who owned the dairy on the left, is on the right in the doorway. The pastry cook and steam bakery cart belonged to Percy Selwyn, whose baker's shop is in the background beside the parked bicycle.

The Byes, Sidmouth, c.1925. Note the novel (and cheap) bridge.

The River Sid at the bottom of Lymbourne Road in 1924.

Sidmouth High Street around the turn of the century. The old thatched cottages were demolished soon after the picture was taken. Today Potbury's showrooms occupy the site.

High Street, Sidmouth, c.1884, when Potbury & Sons were still trading as Farrant. One wonders what today's traffic warden would make of a horse 'parked' outside the shops! There was to be considerable change on the left-hand side of the street during the next two decades. By 1905 (see p.32) Farrant's had grown another storey and the bay window been changed into a shop; the ivy-clad house beyond Farrant's had changed into two shops, and the rather solid-looking house beyond that became first the Devon & Cornwall bank and today is Lloyds.

Fore Street, Sidmouth, c.1905. J. Lake & Son's omnibus office is on the right just beyond the tobacconists, with C.A. Maeer's dairy on the immediate left. Next again is Trumps Stores.

High Street, Sidmouth, c.1905. The entrance to the Methodist Church can just be seen on the left. Erected in 1885, the chapel was considerably rebuilt and added to in 1964, the door just visible ceasing to exist. But to older Sidmouthians the main interest in this picture will be the white building in the centre, part of Union Court, which was knocked down to make room for the Grand Cinema, changed to tearooms after its partial destruction by fire in the 1950s (see p.8).

The Esplanade and Bedford Hotel, Sidmouth, c.1905.

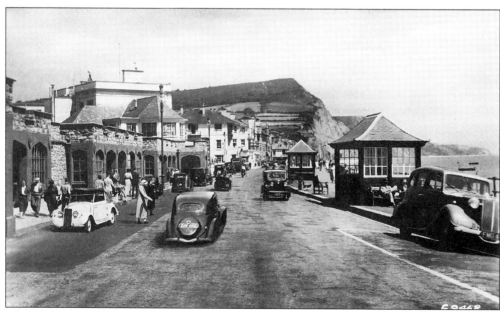

The Esplanade, Sidmouth, looking east from below the Fortfield cricket field, c.1939. It is interesting to note just how much the motor car had taken over in the thirty-odd years since the top picture was taken.

The Esplanade, Sidmouth, called 'The Promenade' on this card sent to Warwick during World War One, which dates it to around 1914.

The western end of the Esplanade, Sidmouth, at the turn of the century, showing one of the town's handsome gas lights.

SOUVENIR BOOK

of the Dedication of

The Connaught Gardens
Sidmouth.

Price 6d.

Sidmouth was *en fête* on 3 November 1934 when Field Marshall HRH The Duke of Connaught dedicated The Connaught Gardens before a large crowd including the full Council under its chairman Councillor George Saunders, JP. A limekiln had originally stood on this site and old prints indicate that there had also once been a cottage here. Later a house known as Sea View was built and, although both it and its grounds were more or less derelict by the time the property was purchased by the Sidmouth Urban District Council, many of the stoutly built garden walls and outhouses were dovetailed into the design of the shelters and the covered walks. Also many of the trees and shrubs of the old garden, including Camillas, Ilex and Tamarix, were retained. The great day began at 11.30 a.m. with Sidmouth Town Prize Silver Band playing the National Anthem prior to the Royal Duke's being received by the Chairman of the Council and presented to the more important people present. He then performed the Dedication Ceremony, dedicated the Grounds and unveiled the tablet. Prior to all this the waiting crowds had been entertained by the Town Band.

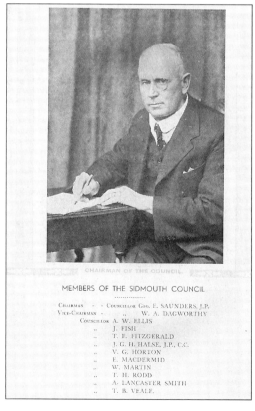

CHAIRMAN OF THE COUNCIL

MEMBERS OF THE SIDMOUTH COUNCIL

Chairman - - Councillor Geo. E. SAUNDERS, J.P.
Vice-Chairman - ,, W. A. DAGWORTHY
Councillor A. W. ELLIS
,, J. FISH
,, T. E. FITZGERALD
,, J. G. H. HALSE, J.P., C.C.
,, V. G. HORTON
,, E. MACDERMID
,, W. MARTIN
,, T. H. RODD
,, A. LANCASTER SMITH
,, T. B. VEALE.

The Bangor class minesweeper HMS *Sidmouth* was completed in March 1941, with the town raising £160,000 towards its cost. The vessel served until 1951, when it was broken up at Charleston, USA.

THE BRIDGE, SIDMOUTH.

The Alma Bridge, Sidmouth, c.1926. This is the second bridge to span the mouth of the Sid, the original being built to shorten the walk to Salcombe Regis in 1855, and it took its name from the Crimean War battle of that name (in 1854) at which the British, French and Turkish forces defeated the Russians during the Crimean War. The second bridge was constructed in 1900.

The Torbay Hotel, Sidmouth, c. 1955.

Sidmouth Beach, c.1888. Although a watering place of considerable repute since the Napoleonic Wars, Sidmouth was also still very much a fishing town when this picture was taken. Was it the wish to maintain the town's 'genteel' air, or had no one as yet realised the advertising potential of the sides of the bathing machines in which modest bathers changed? And was it that 'genteel' reputation that led the errand boy on the right to wear a natty deerstalker, or was he just dressing up for the picture?

This view of St Giles and St Nicholas's church from Sidmouth's Esplanade, taken at the turn of the century, is no longer possible, the gap in the middle of the houses to the left of the Bedford Hotel having been filled in, first by the Western Garage and later by housing.

A sports meeting at Sidmouth's Fortfield cricket ground in 1898. It is not known whether the event is staged by the cricket club. The lonely looking cottage in the background, now the Fort Cafe, was, according to Anna Sutton in her *Story of Sidmouth*, once two small cottages known as both Fortfield Cottages and Fort Cottage. Fortfield itself takes its name from a small fort erected there during the Napoleonic Wars which was demolished before 1836.

Storm damage to Sidmouth's Esplanade during the winter of 1925-26.

Of special interest here, apart from the floods, is Sidmouth's old cinema, which was in the former Belle Vue Restaurant in Fore Street until 1929, when the Grand Cinema was opened.

The Triangle (also known as the Three Cornered Plot), Sidmouth, c.1935.

Clifton Place Private Hotel and Clifton Place, Sidmouth, c.1935. Clifton Place was formerly called Heiffer's Row after a local fisherman who had the houses built. At the time of this picture, which appeared in the 1936 Sidmouth Guide, Clifton Place Hotel was run by its resident proprietress Mrs E.A. Sellek and it offered 'special quotations for winter visits' with 'Electric Light in all bedrooms and bathrooms'.

Duchess of Devonshire ashore at Sidmouth.

The *Duke of Devonshire* shortly after it was grounded in 1934. The paddle steamer, which was built by R.&H. Green of London, was beached while attempting to land passengers at Sidmouth on 27 August 1934.

The *Duchess of Devonshire* was a 230-ton paddle excursion steamer owned by the South Devon and West Bay Steamship Company which plied between Plymouth and Bournemouth calling at such places as Sidmouth, Seaton and Lyme Regis. On 27 August 1934 it sailed from Torquay at 10.30 a.m., with only forty-five passengers because of the wind and the rain which made it bad for cruising. It reached Sidmouth just after 12.30 p.m. but, in order to land her passengers, she had to approach the shore bow end first. When doing so an anchor rope broke and she was swept broadside against the shore where she remained until broken up.

Curious onlookers view the ill-fated steamer.

The crew of the *Duchess of Devonshire*, c.1910.

The Mill Ford, Sidmouth, c.1950. The cyclist seems to prefer his chances in the river rather than use the pedestrian's footbridge.

Sidmouth's Victoria Cottage Hospital, seen here around 1930, was built at the turn of the century and, with her blessing, named after the Queen.

Sidmouth Esplanade looking west from above Alma Bridge, c.1930.

Amyat Place (now Amyatt's Terrace) and St Giles and St Nicholas's church, Sidmouth, from a nineteenth-century print. The terrace was built for Sir John Kennaway by John Amyatt to hide the churchyard, the view of which he disliked intensely.

The Market and Market Post Office, Sidmouth, c.1939.

The Esplanade and the Royal York Hotel, Sidmouth, c.1904. Of special interest here is the 'guide' light for fishing boats, with its ladder and mini-platform for cleaning, priming and lighting the lamp.

Decorations for George VI's Coronation celebrations in Sidmouth's Fore Street in 1937.

Livonia Bridge over the River Sid, Sidmouth, c.1906.

Jacob's Ladder, Sidmouth, c.1910.

Sidmouth Railway Station, c.1931. The railway reached Sidmouth on 6 July 1874 from the former Ottery Road station which then changed its name to Sidmouth Junction. Beeching closed the branch line and the junction but the latter has since re-opened as Feniton station.

The Esplanade, Sidmouth, c.1905.

The Esplanade, Sidmouth, some thirty years after the picture above, when the Mocha Cafe had appeared.

Sidmouth Esplanade, c.1890.

Arch to mark the Duke of Connaught's visit, c.1930.

Cambridge Terrace, Sidmouth, c.1910.

Pebble Cottage, on the corner of Seafield Road and Station Road, Sidmouth, c.1908.

Potbury & Sons, furnishers, auctioneers and house agents and valuers, High Street, Sidmouth, 1899.

High Street, Sidmouth, c.1905. This picture, which was taken by A.L. Sellek, a well-known and, according to him, 'artistic' photographer who lived at 2 Lawn Vista, is of interest, showing as it does two of Sidmouth's old businesses whose premises would later be acquired by Potbury & Sons, the furnishers, just visible on the left. E.T. Sellek, (a relation of the photographer ?), was an ironmonger; Caite & Berwick were milliners. On the right, the Devon and Cornwall Bank is today's Lloyds.

Two

Sidmouth
The People

A crowded Sidmouth Parade listens to the Proclamation of King George V on 9 May 1910.

Sidmouth Girl Guides, taking part in the procession which formed part of Sidmouth's celebrations to mark the Silver Jubilee of King George V in 1935, pass the Faulkner Private Hotel on the Esplanade.

Sidmouth Girl Guide bellringers, c.1943. Left to right: Anne Locke, Sheila Westlake, Sheila Parrish (who moved to Australia), Marion Davis, Mavis Connett.

The parade to mark Queen Victoria's Golden Jubilee in 1887 seems to contain more participants than spectators along the decorated Esplanade. The buildings in the left background above (at the corner of Prospect Place) were opened in 1805 as sea-water baths; part of the premises later became the Mocha Cafe and are still used as such today. Of special interest are the cottage gardens, long-since gone, that front on to the Esplanade. In the bottom picture, where the military are passing, the RNLI flag can be seen on the beach. Sidmouth had two lifeboats; the first, the *Remington*, was launched in 1869; the *William and Francis* arrived in 1891 but was taken out of service in 1910.

Ben Woolley, a member of a prominent Sidmouth fishing family, outside the Fort Cafe in around 1910. Ben was an outstanding rugby player with Sidmouth and Plymouth Albion, and was capped by Devon.

Charabancs operated out of their Western Garage premises by the Sidmouth Motor Company and Dagworthy's Ltd were highly popular in the 1920s and 1930s, especially on the short trips they ran to the top of Salcombe and Peak Hills. This picture was taken around 1926. Note the lady in the front row with a cigarette in her mouth. One of the old charabancs is now at Bicton Gardens near East Budleigh; another at the Beaulieu Motor Museum.

Sidmouth Bird Fanciers Club, 19 November 1937. Mr Perrett is second left, Charles Green in the centre.

Field Marshall HRH The Duke of Connaught took a wide interest in all aspects of Sidmouth's life, including, as seen here in around 1935, the local Bird Fanciers Club.

Miss Hayward, long-serving superintendent at F.W. Woolworth & Co. Ltd's Sidmouth branch, at a presentation to mark her twenty-one years' service, receives an award from Mr Cuss (manager).

Dr Gerald Gibbens, GP at Sidmouth for some forty years, and his family pictured in around 1954 on the scaffolding erected when their Fair Lawn home in Elysian Fields was found to be unsafe. Left to right: Mrs Dierdre Gibbens (a Sidmouth councillor), Jane, Declan, Barney, Dr Gibbens.

Armistice Day, Sidmouth, 1920. This was almost certainly combined with the unveiling of the war memorial, which later moved to the parish church. Note the absence of any development on the Three Cornered Plot.

HRH The Duke of Connaught at what is most likely an Armistice Day Parade in Sidmouth during the early 1930s. Among those who can be seen are Gertie Fry, Mr Irish, Mr Turner and Mr Pratt.

Dr Pullin, who seemed to need little excuse to shin up the tower at Sidmouth's St Giles and St Nicholas's church, was particularly active around the time of the Boer War (1899-1902). He can be seen (above, left) hoisting the Royal Standard (incorrectly as Queen Victoria was nowhere near Sidmouth) on the tower on 6 June 1900, on receipt of the following information from Lord Roberts to Secretary of State for War: 'Pretoria, Tuesday, June 5th, 1900 (11.40am). We are now in possession of Pretoria. The official entry will be made at 2 o'clock this afternoon.' Below, he hoists the Standard, 'with hearty cheers from the Ringers and crowd below', at 8.00a.m. on 2 June 1902. The Boer War peace treaty had been signed at Pretoria by Lords Kitchener and Milner and thirteen Boer delegates at 10.30 p.m. on Saturday 31 May. The news was received in Sidmouth by telephone at 7.30p.m. the following day.

Sidmouth bellringers, c.1957. Back row, left to right: the Lindsey brothers, Ernest Rowe, Alan Mingo, Colin Turner. Middle: Christine Rowe, Jill Smith, Mr Hammett. Front: Marion Davis, Fay Farthing, Percy Davis (captain 1945-87).

Cheers. A fishing trip off Sidmouth in 1938. Left to right: Bill Woolley, a visitor, Billy Burgoyne, landlord of the Marine during the 1930s, another visitor, 'Nobby' Thomas, home on leave from the RAF, and Reg 'Jammy' Woolley.

Theophilus Carslake Mortimore, Sidmouth's last town crier, took up the position in 1924, succeeding his father Theo (see below).

Theo 'Toff' Mortimore, Sidmouth Town Crier, c.1910.

Armistice Day Service (now Remembrance Sunday) at the War Memorial at St Nicholas's church, Sidmouth, just after World War Two.

Founder members at the opening of Sidmouth Bowling Club at their Bedford Lawn Ground on the Esplanade (now the Bedford Car Park) in 1907. Back row, left to right: Mr Percy, W. Burgoin, E. Horton, F. Bartlett, F. Tate, A. Driver, S. Wright, H. Fry, H. Buttle, E. Lake, L. Lake, J. Skinner, W. Weeks, J. Perperell, R. Simmonds, Mr Miller. Second row: Mrs Burgoin, Mrs L. Lake, Mrs E. Lake, Mrs R. Lake, Mrs J. Skinner, Colonel Balfour, Mrs Balfour, Major Hastings, Mrs Hastings, Miss Hastings, Mrs F. Tate, Mrs Pemberthy, Mr Pemberthy. Front: T. Neale, F. Darke, T. Elkins, R. Russell, B. Goss, R. Lake (Sidmouth's surveyor), Mr Mitchell. Mr R.C. Leslie is looking over the fence from the cricket field.

Sidmouth Town Band pictured beside the ruins of the old chancel in 1862.

Sidmouth Town Band pictured at Beer Regatta in 1938. Back row, left to right: G. Reed, M. Gooding, S. Rowlands, J. Elliott, R. Pinney, R. Pinn, -?-, G. Derbyshire, E. Dommett. Middle: F. White, -?-, W. Peacock, N. Newbury, J. Curtis, W. Reed, -?-, T. Jones, W. Gooding, B. Carnell. Front: F. Davey, E. Gooding, L. Glade, R.W. Davison, W. Pring, R. Ellis, G. Burroughs.

Sidmouth Carnival, c.1920, with a tableau entered and manned by staff of Potbury & Sons, the High Street auctioneers and furnishers.

The Manor Court Leet, c.1910. 'Toff' Mortimore, the town crier is on the extreme left, his son Theophilus, who succeeded him, on the extreme right. Also in the picture are Jim Skinner, Farrant Sansom and Harry Fry.

Market Place, Sidmouth, decorated for the coronation of Queen Elizabeth II in 1953.

Orchard Close, Sidford. A Coronation street party in 1953.

Primley Road residents may have had worries about the weather. They held their Coronation street party indoors.

Like so many of the street parties at the time, Sid Road's went on well into the night.

Cutting the cake at Arcot Road's 1953 Coronation street party.

Salters Meadow's Coronation street party.

The older generation were not forgotten at Manstone Square's street party in 1953.

But neither were the Manstone children.

Opening Roxburgh
Flats, c.1955.

Mrs Barrie laying the foundation stone for the Methodist Hall in Church Lane in 1966. The
modernized church was opened by Mrs B. Sanders, whose family originally had the garden on
which the hall now stands.

50

Three
At Work...

It may or may not be true that 'elephants never forget.' But it is highly unlikely that the small boy excitedly pedalling his trike ever forgot this day in the 1950s when the circus marched up Sidmouth's High Street.

International Stores, Fore Street, Sidmouth, c.1905. Formerly the Star Supply Store, the premises are now occupied by the Midland Bank.

VE Day decorations at Anstis Shop, Woolbrook, Sidmouth, in May 1945. The popular butcher and grocery shop was started in 1936 by Tom Anstis, and is today run by the third generation of his family. The cottages bear the date 1709.

A 3d. and 6d. store might not have been in keeping with some people's idea of Sidmouth's undoubted superior status, but, in 1937, F.W. Woolworth & Co. Ltd arrived in the town's High Street. The firm have played an important part in Sidmouth's economic life ever since. The top picture shows the site just after the demolition of the buildings which were sold to the chain store; the lower picture shows the finished job shortly after its opening. The window display certainly appears to have attracted attention despite the long ladder left by the builders or a window cleaner (?). No doubt it is merely coincidence that the right-hand neighbour wants to move out just as Woolworth moves in. Today it is Sue's Pantry and the Tile & Pine Shop.

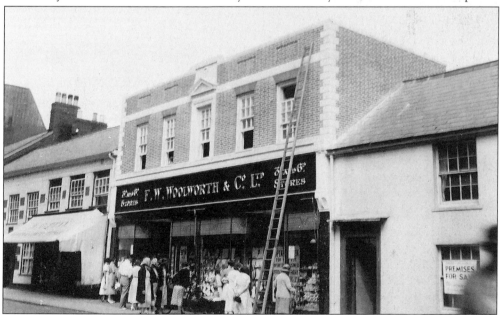

Summers's Royal Dairy, All Saints Road, Sidmouth, c.1900. Today the right-hand (shop) half of the building is a book shop; the left-hand side has become a hairdressers. Later, Mr Summers, whose son runs Sidford Service Station (see p. 76), changed to butchering, although it would seem by the boards above the shop (see below) that he continued the dairy side as well. He increased the window frontage and also included an abattoir at the rear. Of interest to modern Sidmouthians will be the retention of the old butcher's hooks in the wall to the side of today's book shop.

Founded in 1887 by William J. Collier (right), the Church Street furnishing business is still in the family's hands today, William's son William Edward (left) having been succeeded by his son Noel. At one time oil was sold on the premises, and anyone purchasing lino (in the porch) had it measured and cut outside in Church Street, where it frequently fought a losing battle with passing carts.

Harris's 1904 Christmas display. Two points of immediate interest about the Church Street butchers shop are, first, the outside display which, although still fairly common after World War Two, would hardly bring a festive smile to the face of today's Health Inspectors and, secondly, the complete absence of poultry, explained by the fact that Harris was a butcher and sold red meat as opposed to a poulterer who sold poultry. Harris's was bought in 1907 by John James Hayman, who was followed by his son Stanley John. The popular business is still in the Hayman family's hands and is run by John James's grandson, Clive Lewis John.

C.E. Green's fruiterer and florist shop in Sidmouth's Fore Street in the 1950s. The business was started by Mrs Middleton as a grocery, sweet and vegetable shop at the end of World War One, her brother-in-law, Charles Green, taking over in 1923. The shop, now concentrating on being a florist, is run today by Charles' son John. Of interest is 'Nite 513', below the old-style, three-figure Sidmouth telephone number, the spelling InterFlora insisted on for their numbers.

Clarke's shop at Milton House, High Street, Sidmouth, c.1899. Sadly, with the top of the house having undergone considerable alteration, the bust of Milton is no longer to be found, while the premises are now occupied by Stagg's and Feathers.

Sidmouth Post Office, Vicarage Road, Christmas 1955. The post office, now a few yards down the road at Ford's shop, was built in 1938 by Pinney, the local builder. This picture, taken at 12.55 a.m. during the Christmas rush, shows, left to right: Mike Harris, Walter Wagstaffe, Alan Mingo, Dennis Gosling, Fred Lee, Eddy Hart.

Workshop staff of Potbury & Sons, the High Street auctioneers and furnishers, 1906. Back row, left to right: C.J. Thomas, D. Ferns, F. Carter, E. Purchase, A. Lovering. Front: F. Otton, -?-, B. Copp (foreman), C. Hill. Although not a dirty job, it is still interesting to note that all the men are wearing collars and ties.

Potbury & Sons' workshops, High Street, Sidmouth, c.1900.

Waterworks extension, Pin Hill, Sidmouth, 1894.

ELLIOTT BREACH,

Practical Mechanical Engineer,

HOLMDALE, HIGH ST., SIDMOUTH.

(Late L.N.W. Railway Works, Crewe, and Wolseley-Siddeley, Manchester.)

Motor Repairs and Overhauls a Speciality.

Parts Duplicated.

Accessories.

Vulcanizing.

Accumulators charged and repaired.

Official Repairer to R.A.C.

See "Autocar" Directory.

Repairs generally to all kinds of Machinery.

Electric Lighting in all its branches.

TO MOTOR BUYERS.—Before buying, consult us. We are experts, and our advice is free. We will give you sound advice—where and what to buy.

IF HYGIENE, ECONOMY, BEAUTY, AND SIMPLICITY enter into your calculations when you study your house lighting problem, consult ELLIOTT BREACH, Holmdale, SIDMOUTH.

Agent for the CRYPTO ELECTRICAL Co., London.

We have had a large experience in this class of work, and aim at efficiency and economy.

Estimates Free.

We supply Electric Light Generating Plants, &c.

SAVE MONEY BY CONSULTING

ELLIOTT BREACH, *Motor Specialist and Practical Mechanical Engineer,* SIDMOUTH.

TELEPHONE: 60, SIDMOUTH.   TELEGRAMS: "BREACH, SIDMOUTH."

This advert for Elliott Breach, the High Street electrical engineers, dates from around 1905, a time when, along with Sidmouth in general, they were moving into the motor age. Electric lighting was still rare enough at the time for them to mention that all their branches had it.

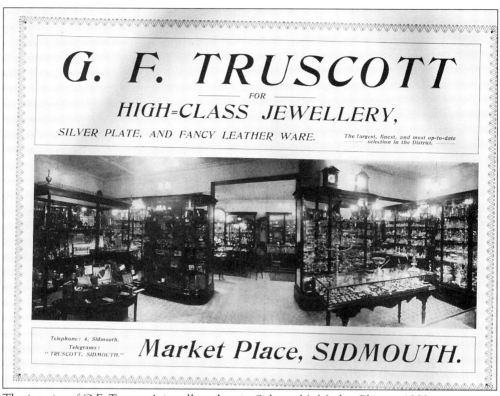

The interior of G.F. Truscott's jewellery shop in Sidmouth's Market Place, c.1908.

Slade & Sons' Garage, Salcombe Road, Sidmouth, c.1958.

Four

... and Play

Sidmouth Sailing Club, c. 1950. Back row, left to right: K. Gardiner, J. Banton, R. Pinney, A. Russell, J. Luxton, A. St G. Lister, L. Beavis, M. Mortimore, A. Fearns, A.D. Gamble. Middle: H. Fish, D. Banton, S. French, J. Mortimore, C. Clarke, R. Harris, A. Bagwell, E. Westlake, A. Beech, R. Northcott, S. Nice. Front: Mrs N. Govier, N. Govier, G. Bastin, E. Purchase, S. Williams, G. Channing (commodore), W.J. Beavis, S.T. Chard, R. Fish, Mrs G. Channing.

The pictures on this and the opposite page have been selected not only to show Carnivals in the 1950s, but also because they offer a glimpse of Sidmouth businesses no longer with us, such as MacFisheries, when it was at the lower end of Old Fore Street in 1958.

Just around the corner from MacFisheries in New Street, also in 1958, are Belle Vue Dairy and Eric Castle's photographer's shop.

Of interest here in Vicarage Road (in 1952 – when it rained a lot!), especially to those Sidmouthians who can remember the town during World War Two, will be the old British Canteen on the extreme right, where, during the war, it was possible to enjoy an off-ration cooked dinner for as little as a shilling. Today the Catholic Church Hall occupies the site, while Reed Motors is now ATS Tyres.

A few yards down the road in the mid-1950s was the popular Harolds, the gents and sportwear outfitters, at what was then Cavendish House. This is today's C&C Electrical, run by equally popular couple Carlton and Barbara Leworthy.

Sidmouth Parish Bell Ringers, Armistice Day, 11 November 1918. Back row, left to right: T. Fouracre, W. Stoneman, A.B. Webber, W.G. Conant, W. Perry. Front: W. Oldrey, J.B. Coldwill (capt), J. Farrant.

Sidmouth Rugby Football Club, 1887. Back row, left to right: D. Pullin, F.J. Potbury, W.A. Thornton, B. Pullin. Middle row: T. Selley, C. Thornton, R. Clarke, H.T. Bolt (in hat). Front: W. Skinner, W. Pideley, H. Taylor, R. Soloman, R. Potbury, W. Potbury, J. Bolton, J. Bartlett.

Edwardian rugby at Coburg Field, Sidmouth.

Sidmouth Rugby Football Club pictured in 1930 prior to a game which was played in the presence of HRH The Duke of Connaught, Queen Victoria's son and a frequent visitor to the town. Back row, left to right: G. Bolt, G.A. Thomas, J. Mills, E.O. Smith, F. Davey, Dr B. Pullin, E. Pike, P. Fitzgerald, F. Ellis, T. Fitzgerald. Middle: G. Carter, E. Channing, R. Blake, B. Welsman, E. Pyne, B. Turner. Front: W. Harris, R. Knapp (capt).

Sidmouth Cricket Club 2nd XI, winners of the County Cup in 1937. Back row, left to right: H.A. Pickson (sec), L.T. Stamp, J.T. O'Brien, F.A. Coles, W.A. Aldridge, G.B. Carter, H. Tozer (scorer). Front: G.L. Maeer, R.J. Courtney, W.A. Fish (capt), G.R.Fisher (vice-capt), E.G. Pyne, E.S. Badcock.

Sidmouth Lawn Tennis Club, 1929. Left to right: H.V. Newton (Men's Championship runner-up, 1926 and 1929), Capt Ashton, J.F.G. Lysaght, E.C. Peters (Men's Championship winner 1927, 1928, 1929).

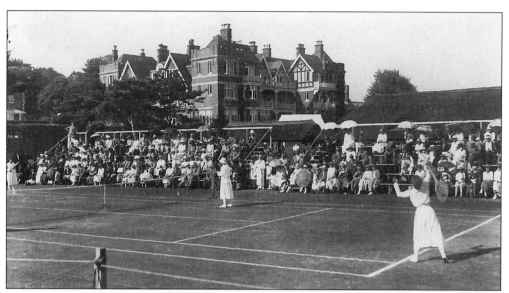

A tennis tournament at Fortfield in the early 1920s. In those days the big tournaments attracted many well-known players to Sidmouth and all Sidmouth's 'society', whether they knew anything about the game or not, thronged the ground to watch.

Sidmouth Cricket Club, 1936. Back row, left to right: F.C. Hopwood, Capt E. Capel, Admiral Silk CBE, A.F. Irish, G.L.C. Maeer, E. Badcock, R.J. Courtney, R. Grattan (score-boy), F. Fowler (scorer), E.R. Channing (umpire). Front: R. Prendergast, K.S. Dabiell, E.A. Fulcher, H.E. Skinner (capt), A.G. Skinner (vice-capt), E.E. Whitton, E. Breach.

Sidmouth Carnival passes the old Post Office in Vicarage Street, 1960.

Gliddon's entry in Sidmouth's 1959 Carnival.

Proudly carrying her first prize card, a 1950s fancy dress entrant passes the Mocha Cafe on the Esplanade

At the other end of the Esplanade, also in the 1950s, the parade passes the former Burgoynes Coach Tours office.

Sidmouth Amateur Dramatic Society's 1958 production of *The Blind Goddess*. Left to right: Gillian Beatty, David Pook, Eileen McKenna, Peter James, Nella Allen, Enid Temple-Cotton, Douglas Whitehall, Peter Hall.

Sidmouth Amateur Dramatic Society's 1956 production of *Uncertain Jury*. Eileen McKenna is on the left, Alex Lewis on the right. The society was founded in 1922, although in her excellent book *A Story of Sidmouth*, Anna Sutton places its first meeting in the Manor Hall in January 1923, its subsequent first production being *Tilly of Bloomsbury*. It moved into its present home in Woolcombe Hall in the Byes (on the site of the old Sea Scouts' hut erected during World War One) in the early 1950s.

VE Day Party (May 1945) in Sidmouth's Brewery Lane.

Sidmouth Rugby Club, 1895-96, the side that created the (then) record of winning the Devon Junior and Senior Challenge Cups in successive seasons under the captaincy of W.C. Vallance. Back row, left to right: H. Culverwell (sec), H.S. Potbury, H. Channing, H. Skinner, R. Youldon, T. Woolley, J. Skinner (touch judge). Middle: T. Fitz-Gerald, P. Baron, W.C. Vallance, W. Skinner, W. Poulton, T. Russell, I. MacDonald. Front: S. Skinner, A. Skinner, G. Berry, F. Skinner. On their return from the Senior Cup Final the team (seen above) was pulled around the town with the cup to the strains of 'See The Conquering Hero Comes'.

Sidmouth Golf Club's club house, c.1906. Like so many others, the Sidmouth club has just celebrated its centenary. It was founded in 1889 when a tiny, thatched club house was built; this was replaced by the building seen here in 1905.

Sidmouth boys' rugby team (1913-14) which won the cup presented by Dr Pullin for boys' rugby. Among those present are local postman Fred Pound (with the stick, on the left of the back row), 'Fairy' Purchase, Eric Mills, 'Smut' Salter, Jim Burgoyne, Lloyd Burgoyne, 'Bengy' Weeks and Billy Burgoyne, the mascot in front with the cup.

Five
Sidford and Sidbury

The Sidford-based coal merchants and hauliers, Perry Bros (see p.82), was started around 1920 in Fry's Lane on what was originally an orchard and a tennis court. Among their earlier ventures was the coach seen here outside the Poltimore Arms at Pinhoe, and presumably taking a party from Sidford or Sidmouth on an outing.

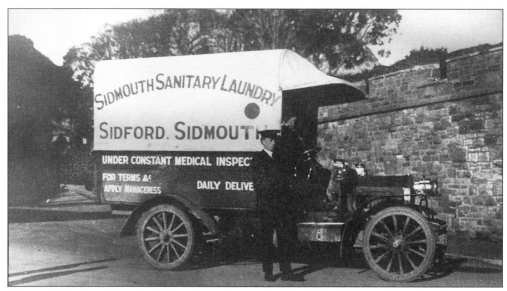

Sidmouth Sanitary Laundry is thought to have existed in Sidford from at least the closing years of the nineteenth century, probably even earlier, and by the time of the above picture, which was taken just before World War One, had moved from collections by horse and cart and hand-drawn barrows into the motor age. Of particular interest is the claim that the laundry was 'under constant medical inspection'. Around 1910, and for reasons not now known, it was employing several women from Brittany, and a dispute between these and management led to several female workers leaving and forming a rival laundry, the Victoria Steam Laundry, in a field next door known as Pig Orchard. The picture below shows workers at the new laundry, of a type known as a 'hand laundry', soon after it began operations. The premises seen here, although now enlarged and modernised, are still part of the present laundry's buildings. In 1939 Mrs Ruth Hargreaves bought the business which remains in the family's hands today. The Sidmouth Laundry was finally bought out by the 'newcomers'.

Church Street, Sidford, looking west, c.1939.

The old pack-horse bridge over the River Sid (previously the 'ford' from which Sidford takes it name). Seen here at the turn of the century, the tiny, twelfth-century bridge was far too narrow for the increasing traffic after World War One, and it was widened in 1930. Happily, authority retained the old bridge and incorporated it in the pedestrian path at the side of the modern bridge.

Mr Summers's old garage (left) at the junction of Sidford's School Street and High Street seen here around 1938.

The old Tourist Rest (also called the Cyclists' Rest) at the Cross Roads, Sidford, seen here just after World War Two, was an attractive and popular old tea house run at the time of this photograph by Mrs Stevens. It lost much of the left-hand half in the interest of road safety in around 1960, the rest gradually vanishing to make room for expansion by the next-door Sidford Service Station.

Like the cattle below, the East Devon Hunt would not be as welcome today outside the Rising Sun in Sidford's School Street as it was here in around 1929.

Church Street, Sidford, c.1951, before the Hamilton Garage (on the left) lost its roadside petrol pumps and moved the workshops to the rear. Applegarth (on the right) is still a guest house and restaurant, now known as the Salty Monk. Imagine the traffic jam if Farmer Dyer's cows were herded along the busy A3502 road today.

Sidford School, c.1925. Back row, left to right: Miss Gale, Sydney Vinnicombe, -?-, Lucy Dean, Harry Layzell, Willie Vinnicombe, Rene Kellian. Middle: Mary Clark, Phylis Gosling, Gladys Bottomley, Raymond Quick, Cyril Pollard, Mollie Kellian. Front: Joyce Irish, Edna Irish, Roy Northcott, Billy Morrish, Sammy Hooper.

School Street, Sidford, c. 1938. Sidford's post office has moved further along the road (approximately where the lorry is parked); Warner's shop has become three separate businesses: Andrea's hairdressers, Vinnicombe's bakery and Fern's greengrocers.

The Rising Sun, School Street, Sidford, c.1938.

Incorrectly called Seaton Road on this late 1930s postcard, the view is of Church Street, Sidford. The ivy-covered house on the right is now Hendy's newsagents; the barn in the centre, part of Myrtle Farm, is now the Spar shop.

The Blue Ball, Sidford, c.1936. The brick-built St Mary's church in the background was erected in 1873 and, although it might fail to excite the over-demanding school that thinks 'only old is beautiful', it is a charming building.

Around 1960 a lorry lost its brakes descending Trow Hill into Sidford and crashed into Mr Lockyer's coal lorry, which was making a delivery to the Blue Ball Inn, shed its load of pipes, and caused considerable damage to both vehicles.

The Cross, Sidford, c.1910. Mainly residential at the time of this photograph, the junction of the Exeter and Sidmouth roads now constitutes Sidford's shopping centre.

High Street, Sidford, c.1954. The barn on the extreme left, then part of Myrtle Farm, is now a supermarket.

William Henry Perry, who once ran today's Davey's butchers shop in Sidford, began his coal and general hauliers business in Frys Lane around 1920. His sons, Frederick John and Leonard Charles, took over after World War Two, and the business is still in family hands. Leonard's son Barry and daughter-in-law Marion are in charge.

Sidford Minature Rifle Club in 1911, when they won the Morrison Bell Cup given for annual competition to rifle clubs in his Honiton constituency by MP Clive Morrison Bell. It is interesting to note that shooting was not thought 'ungenteel' for the fair sex. Back row, left to right: Mr S. White, Mr W. Hugh, Mr F. Morrish, Mr W. Morrish, Mr A. Morrish. Front: Miss Helman, Mr Lang, Miss Bolt.

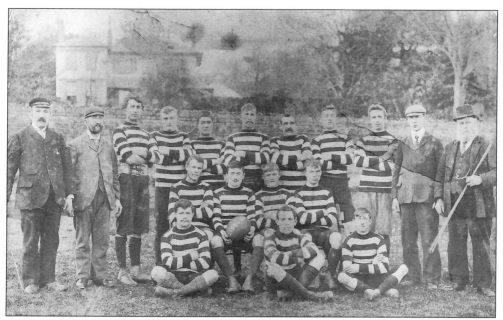

Sidbury Rugby Club, 1902-03. Unfortunately, only the names of the back row are known. They are, left to right: A.W.R. Taylor, J. Headington (sec), A. Pike, G. Richards, J. Newbery, J. Domond, C. Pinn, W. Morrish, H. Baker, E. Brown, J. Purchase (touch judge). The latter, complete with long-handled flag, hardly looks dressed for the part.

Sidbury School football 1st XI, 1929-30. Back row, left to right: Perry, Arthur Hartnell, Bill Hull, Archie Fowler, Mr Marcom (head), Lane, Bert Melluish, Percy Churchill, Donald Aplin. Middle: Dick Matthew, Fred Elliott, Tom Summers, Walter Pike, Lloyd Pike. Front: John Cordey.

Sidbury School, c.1933. Maria Greenfield, -?-, Arnold Enticott, Freda Clay, Doreen Richards, Miss Summers. Middle: -?-, Dora Pring, Florrie Pinn, Rosaline Pring, Myrtle Spiller, Alec Taylor, Brian King. Front: Gerald Snell, Jean Mitchell, Sheila Hartnoll, Vincent, Derek Solman, Eileen Pike, -?-.

Sidbury School, c.1954. Back row, left to right: Elizabeth Pinn, -?-, Wendy Broomfield, -?-, -?-. Second row: Bob Denning, -?-, -?-, -?-, Sheila Quick, Christine Pinn, Valerie Pring, John Lamb, Keith Maeer, Anthony Selway. Third row: Raymond Melluish, Malcolm Sweet, Syd Pring, David Baldwin, Raymond Vincent, Les Cole, Malcolm Eveleigh, Jack Taylor.

The Bakery, Sidbury, c.1900. No longer thatched, and without the tall and rather dangerous-looking chimney, this was in recent years a tea room.

Bridge Street, Sidbury, looking east, c.1926. The handsome, thatched cottages on the left, today sporting equally handsome thatched porches, were saved from demolition in 1939 by the outbreak of World War Two. Fifteen cottages in all were sold by Sidbury Manor for £200 — for the lot, not each! — and scheduled for demolition. Happily, the plans were shelved after the war engaged the builders in more serious matters. One shudders to think, however, what this charming part of a charming village would have looked like had fate not intervened.

Bridge Street, Sidbury, c.1938. Fred Skinner herds his father Dick's cows home to Deepway Farm for milking. Snowball leads the way.

Deepway and Stoney Bridge, Sidbury, c.1909. The thatched cottages behind the bridge were known as 'Part of John's' in the eighteenth and early nineteenth centuries, and were among the many properties in the village owned or rented by members of the Hayman family. The stone building on the extreme left was Sidbury butcher Mr Pike's slaughterhouse. A Mr Taylor who lived in one of the cottages was employed raising and lowering the mill leat. The small thatched house immediately behind the bridge was Mr Coles' cyder house.

The Red Lion, Sidbury, with the Royal Oak in the background, c.1898. The attractive thatched buildings between the two inns were the only ones to escape the ravages of fire in the early nineteenth century. The Royal Oak originally stood a few hundred yards away on the site of the modern Village Hall.

Sidbury village centre and St Giles' church, certainly before 1884 when the 'pepper pot' roof to the tower was replaced by a small spire. Later, to mark Queen Victoria's Jubilee, a drinking fountain and horse trough appeared just to the left of the church gate. St Giles' is certainly among East Devon's better churches, its Roman tower having been accurately rebuilt in 1843. It houses eight bells, the tenor weighing in at over 16cwt; the oldest, the Fourth, dates from 1662.

Sidbury War Memorial soon after its erection in around 1921, and Rose Cottage (right). Today the Furze Hill council house estate has appeared behind the memorial.

Burnt Oak, Sidbury, c.1914, as seen on a Chapman card. Although the Dawlish-based postcard firm did sell the popular tourist views such as sea fronts and churches, they also went to the back streets and less attractive, even ugly, parts of towns, so making themselves invaluable to the local historians who came later. Although Burnt Oak is not ugly, it does have the heavy look associated with much Victorian and Edwardian red-brick architecture. The iron railings went during World War Two salvage drives, but otherwise there is not a lot of change in this detached part of the village, apart from TV aerials and modern doors and windows.

Sidmouth Carnival, c.1959. Sidbury Football Club entry is moving along the sea front.

Sidbury Football Club's tableau at the first Sidmouth Carnival to be held following World War Two, in around 1948. Among those taking part are Bunny Palmer, Jack Selway, Lloyd Pike, Dolwyn Summers and Tom Summers.

Sidmouth Carnival. Among those taking part in Sidbury Football Club tableau entry the 'Moonrackers' in the early 1950s are 'Bunny' Palmer, Delwin Summers, Harry Wood, Bill Maeer and Lloyd Pike.

Sidbury Football Club, c.1948, photographed at their ground at Sidford. Among those seen here are 'Bunny' Palmer, who started the club, Jack Selway, Viv Thorn, Ernie Taylor, Raymond Patch, John Harvey and Norman Taylor.

In around 1958 fourteen Sidbury men came up trumps with a £42,000 win on the pools and celebrated their good fortune at the Royal Oak. Left to right: Des Hull and Ron Cave (rear), Reg Edwards, Francis Pinn, Maurice Reed, Jack Davey, Bert Melluish, Frank Taylor, George Brannan, Vic Quick (piano), Ernie Clay, Tony Myhill, Arthur Pinn, Tom Summers.

Sidbury United AFC, 1948-49. Back row, left to right: G.W. Parsons, E. Northcott, F.A.T. Howell, J. Selway, C.J. Woodley, R.E. West, J.C. Harvey, E.J. Taylor, R.C. Vanstone, H.H. Palmer (chairman), K. Fisher. Front: W. Maeer, J. Marchant, R.E. Gush, F.Barrett, V.A. Thomas (vice-captain), D.L. Fogwill (front with ball), H.J. Boyland, A.E. Summers, G. Spence, H.C. Wood.

Len Lockyer's Albion lorry loaded with logs outside the Royal Oak, Sidbury, c.1949.

Regulars at Sidbury's Royal Oak checking that the quality of the cyder from Sidmouth's Vallance's Brewery is up to its usual high standards in around 1948. Sadly, the Brewery closed towards the end of the 1950s; equally sadly, the Royal Oak closed as recently as 1992. Left to right: Len Lockyer (landlord), -?-, Reg Bargery, Jack Davey, -?-, Norman Taylor, Ernie Clay, Caryl Irish, Sidford's blacksmith Fred Skinner, Jack Keast.

Sir Charles Cave swearing in the jury and officers of Sidbury Court Leet, c.1958. Left to right: Walt Elliott, F.T. Summers, Mr Coles, Mr Hamlin, -?-, Len Lockyer, -?-, Syd Spiller, -?-, -?-, Sir Charles Cave.

Regulars at Sidbury's Royal Oak after demolishing a pile of pennies that reached the ceiling and produced almost £200 for the Blind School at Exeter. Those present include the landlord, Len Lockyer, his wife Joyce (standing behind and right of the coins), Ern Taylor, Mrs Palmer, Mrs Sherwell, Jack Davey, Harry Pinn, Syd King, Tom Summers and Winsome Perry.

Sidbury Harvest Festival sports day, 1908.

Sidbury Church Fête in the Vicarage Gardens, c.1955. Left to right: -?- (in front), Mollie Pike, Sheila Haywood, Hilary Blackmore, ? Jolliffe, Jack Selway, Marion Hallett, Gillian Blackmore, Nellie Driver, -?-, -?-, -?-.

Ern Bourne, Sidbury's blacksmith, in his forge (see below) below the butcher's shop in the 1920s.

The blacksmith's shop, Sidbury, c.1908. It is still there today but now used as a storeroom.

Henry Mellors, carter to Mr Richard King of Buckley Farm, in around 1908. No disrespect to Henry, but no prizes for guessing the stars in this picture.

Children leaving for sports and tea at Sidbury Manor in 1937. Derek King (extreme left), Ike Eveleigh, and one of the Paynes are among those with smiling faces.

Chapel Street, Sidbury, c.1904.

Paradise Row, Sidbury, c.1920. Paradise Row (right) was a row of thatched cottages that ran at right-angles to the road. They were demolished in the 1930s. Myrtle Farm on the left is still with us though, albeit minus the myrtle tree.

Sidbury Fair, seen here in around 1924, began on the second Tuesday of September and was opened by the traditional hoisting of a white glove at noon from the upper windows of the (now sadly closed) Royal Oak. Later, children scrambled for hot pennies thrown from a window of the Red Lion. On the Wednesday there was a cattle, sheep and pig auction, and throughout the fair there were stalls and, as seen above, morris dancing and other country attractions. The end of the fair was signalled by the lowering of the white glove at midnight after a dance.

Sidbury postman Harry Banks delivering telegrams announcing the outbreak of World War One in August 1914 to the Slade's house at the corner of Deepway and Stoney Bridge. Mr Slade, reading the news with obvious concern, was the landlord of the Red Lion.

Sidbury Post Office, c.1910. Harry Banks, on the left with the pony and trap (and dog), obviously did the country rounds. His colleagues are Mr Hook (behind horse) and Mr Bennett, who appears to favour non-regulation headgear and doubled as Town Crier. The boy with the hoop is Stan Skinner.

Sidbury School staff, c.1925. Back row, left to right: Miss Hawkins, Miss Rutherford, Miss Garland. Front row: Miss Webber, Mr Knight (head), Miss Knight.

Sidbury Home Guard, c.1941. Left to right: Sgt 'Bunny' Palmer, Lieutenant Strickland, W. Pike, Cpl D. Finlayson. The platoon had as many as fifty members. This quartet is about to set off on the daily dawn patrol around the hills that surround the village to see if any parachutists have landed. Their specially purchased Armstrong-Siddely car was one of the first automatics.

Six
Branscombe

The wedding of Harry Layzell and Dora Perry at Branscombe in the 1920s. Also present are Dan and Elizabeth Perry, Mr and Mrs Fred Layzell, Annie Layzell, Charles Hawker, Margaret Hawker, Jack Perry and Ivor Collier.

Branscombe's Apple-Pie Fayre is known to date back to at least 1789, when legend has it that the making of small apple pies was an old tradition in the village. The theft of a pie from the vicarage led to the making of a large communal one, which was cut up by the squire, the vicar and the ladies, and handed around. It is also said that the stolen pie was taken to a local fair and paraded around in triumph. Probably the two stories got mixed up down the years. The fair was allowed to lapse in the late 1950s, mainly through the outbreak of foot-and-mouth disease in the village. Happily it was restarted in 1988 but, unhappily, without the old carnival-type procession held on the Saturday night when the village and the pubs, especially the pubs, were crowded. Branscombe was on the Southern National Bus Company's Seaton–Sidmouth route at the time, and the crowds forced the company to cancel all buses during the three-hour period the jollifications lasted. The top picture, from the 1940s or '50s if the clothes are anything to go by, shows the giant apple pie being dragged in triumph through the village; below, and probably pre-war, the cart for the pie is being made up by its 'Wurzel' attendants.

Branscombe's Tudor smithy, sporting at least three blacksmiths when this picture was taken shortly after World War One, is still in use today, although it has lost its trees and a village hall has appeared to its right.

Probably rivalling even St Winifred's as the most photographed building in the village, Branscombe's smithy is of Tudor origins and still in use today – and with a lady blacksmith! This picture, from 1934, shows the then smith Mr Layzell with his son Harry at work on a wheel.

Branscombe, c.1945, from the school.

The old Village Hall, Branscombe, c.1960. Although since replaced by a modern and well-appointed new hall, the former building has a warm spot in most older residents' memories. It was, after all, the focal spot of village life for many years.

Seaside Farm, Branscombe, seen here in around 1908, is a fine Elizabethan building.

Hillside, Branscombe, c.1929. It is often said that Branscombe gets its name from 'branched combe', a clear reference to the two arms of the valley (there is a smaller third) that meet here and run to the sea. More likely, however, it is from 'Branoc's' combe; Branoc was a Celtic saint whose name is also retained in the village in the shape of the popular Branoc's Ale brewed at Seaside Farm (above) and sold at the Fountain Head (see page 107) at the other end of the village.

Branscombe, c.1922.

St Winifred's church, Branscombe, c.1912. Arguably the finest village church in Devon, St Winifred's is an outstanding building with much Norman work, including the sturdy crossing tower. Its unusual dedication is to a little-known seventh-century saint who was loved by Prince Cradocus. When his love was not returned he cut off her head. He immediately dropped dead and the earth opened up and swallowed him. She was restored to life by St Bueno, a health-giving spring spurting from the spot on which her head landed, and she spent her life in the good works which led to her canonisation.

The Fountain Head, Branscombe, seen here in around 1906, is a lovely old pub of indeterminate age at the top of Branscombe, where the Sidmouth road clambers away up the hill. Inside it is all old timbers, stone-flagged floors and mysterious corners.

The Masons Arms, Branscombe, c.1920. Some parts of the old pub, which started life as fishermen's cottages, are said to date from 1400, but it is a mainly seventeenth-century building.

Branscombe School, c.1927.

Otton's Shop, Branscombe Square, c.1904.

The 1st Branscombe Girl Guides help with the village's waste paper collection in 1940. Left to right: Winnie Trivett, Elsie Pittman, Mrs Smith, Edith Self, Ivy Wohlgemuth, Miss Freeman, Joyce Frappell, Doris Whatton. A great emphasis was put on salvage during the war, when not only paper but saucepans and other aluminium articles were much sought after by the authorities. It was at this time that many handsome railings vanished as well.

Branscombe Village Band, c.1904.

Branscombe bell ringers outside St Winifred's church in 1900. Those pictured include Revd Swansborough (rear), Bill Parrot (front row, second left) and Alfred Perryman (standing at the far right).

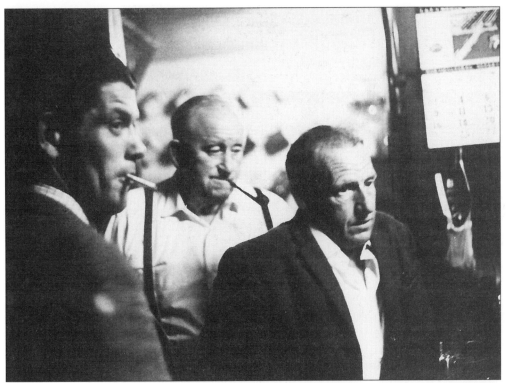

Archie Gill (centre) was popular landlord of Branscombe's Fountain Head Inn for many years and what is known as a 'character'. He is seen here in the bar with two regulars, Stewart Barrett (left) and Dickie Lloynd, in around 1948.

Branscombe Special Constables in 1939. Left to right: Leonard Dowell, Mr Hayman, Lew Perryman, Clement Ford, Bert Somers, Alfred Hutchings, Archie Perryman.

The smiling faces and the empty bottles have no connection, but Branscombe ladies have been celebrating something, possibly to do with the Apple-Pie Fayre, in the 1930s. They are, starting at the back and running left to right: Mrs Kelly, Vera Dowell (in front), Edith Hayman, -?-, Mr Kelly, Emily Perry, Ethel Butters, Florence Payne, Edith Hawker, Rita Smith, Eva Perryman, Mrs Ellis, Madge White, Freda Pollard, Hilda Billson, Ivy Collier, Lily Pike, Florence Perryman.

Mrs Gosling and Clifford Gosling with
the Pinney family (in the donkey cart),
c.1904. The Goslings lived in the higher
of the two cottages seen here, and on the
road that led up from Street, Branscombe,
to Berry Barton.

Apple picking above Lower Deem,
Branscombe, c.1906. Among those shown
are George and Emmanuel Pike, Mildred
Farrant, Marjorie Loveridge and Chris
Butter.

John Gill's shop and the old chapel, Branscombe, c.1902.

Margells Hill and Millers Lea, Branscombe, with the wartime factory in the foreground.

John and Jane Wood of Grapevine, Branscombe, are not going to let a little thing like a snowdrift stop them going to chapel in around 1908.

Grapevine, Branscombe, decorated for George V's Silver Jubilee, 1935. Gladys Woodrow (left) and Rita Abbott (now Saunders) pose outside this attractive part of the sprawling village.

Branscombe's celebrations on the occasion of Edward VII's Coronation in 1902.

The committee which arranged Branscombe's celebrations to mark Queen Victoria's Golden Jubilee in 1887. Back row, left to right: William Farrant, Mr Swansborough, Robert Salter, Mark Henry, William Borough, John Gill, Sam Hill, -?-. Front: B. Dowell, -?-, Mr Clarke, -?-, Henry Pike.

Seven

Newton Poppleford

Newton Poppleford British (later Royal British) Legion's first parade in 1924, headed by the village band, with Syd Knight on the trombone. As they are just about to pass Church Cottages on the extreme left, they are obviously heading for St Luke's church. St Luke's, dating mostly from 1897, was once a chantry of the church of the Blessed Virgin Mary at Aylesbeare, but was separated in 1862.

Newton Poppleford, c.1905. The open ground on the right in front of St Luke's church has since been developed.

The corner of Back Lane and Station Road, Newton Poppleford, c.1938, showing the now-demolished Turk's Head on the right.

The Turk's Head Inn, Newton Poppleford, c.1942. Back row, left to right: Arthur Devereux (landlord), -?-, Bill Wheaton. Front: visitor, visitor, Frances Devereux.

The Turk's Head Inn, demolished during the 1960s, was a casualty of the huge increase in traffic along the then A35 part of the Folkestone–Exeter trunk road; it stuck out into the road and was the cause of many accidents and near misses. This picture from the 1950s must have been taken just after one such accident. The police sergeant appears to be measuring the road.

The Cannon Inn, Newton Poppleford, c.1899.

Mr Willoughby-Smith, who lived at Benshams, was a great benefactor to Newton Poppleford, as well as being the owner of this magnificent coach and four, seen here in the Benshams drive in around 1910.

Newton Poppleford Coronation Pageant, June 1953. The gathering would not be very popular with motorists on today's busy Exeter Road.

The Flurry Dance during the 1955 Newton Poppleford Carnival passes Donnaralle Guest House (opposite the Cannon Inn). Dancers, left to right: -?-, -?-, Mrs Knight, Mrs Vickery, Archie Bastin, Gwen Jones, Marjorie Statham, Rita Wood, Mary Marchant, Gladys French, -?-.

Newton Poppleford railway station, c.1925, with Roberts' coal lorry unloading a coal truck. George Roberts started the family coal business in 1887 when the railway came to Newton Poppleford. He was followed by his son Reg and his grandson Norman. The business was sold in 1970.

Women more than 'Did Their Bit' during World War Two, when thousands took over jobs usually done by the men who were away in the Forces. Here Queenie Roberts (left) and Betty Hill pose for the camera between filling coal bags at Newton Poppleford Station and delivering the coal around the district in Mr Roberts' lorry in 1942.

A Turk's Head outing to the *Babes in the Wood* pantomime at Exeter, c.1935.

Newton Poppleford railway station, c.1964. The Sidmouth branch line was opened on 6 July 1874 with intermediate stops at Ottery St Mary and Tipton St John; the Budleigh Salterton branch from the latter station was opened on 15 May 1897 and had Newton Poppleford among its intermediate stops. It was extended to Exmouth in 1903. Both lines closed to passenger traffic on 6 March 1967.

Newton Poppleford Football Club, c.1929.

Newton Poppleford Football Club's under-14s team receiving the East Devon Youth League's Stanley Cup from the donor Stan Trenchard of Axminster following the final at Axminster Town's Sector ground in around 1958. The league's first secretary, Gerald Gosling, is extreme right.

Although this gentleman's name is not known, it is thought he was a relation of Kelso Mingo. He is pictured here holding the two 56lb weights he carried on his head up the church steps around the turn of the century. It is said he was unable to turn his head for some while afterwards!

A fire in Newton Poppleford's High Street in around 1908.

Haymaking at Benshams, Newton Poppleford, 1912.

The East Devon Hunt move off in Newton Poppleford around 1922.

Newton Poppleford School, 1912.

The Rogation Sunday procession just about to turn into St Luke's church at Newton Poppleford, c.1959.

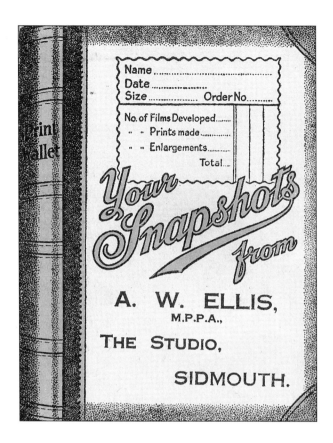

Name ....
Date ....
Size .... Order No ....

No. of Films Developed ....
 " " Prints made ....
 " " Enlargements ....
                            Total ...

Your Snapshots from

A. W. ELLIS,
M.P.P.A.,
THE STUDIO,
SIDMOUTH.

Print
wallet

Acknowledgements

We are particulary grateful to George Tenney for access to his fine collection of Newton
Poppleford material, to Branscombe Parish Council, especially Elsie Mayo (archivist) and Linda
Hughes (clerk), and would like to place on record our appreciation of the way in which that
village has preserved its pictorial past, to Maurice Dunford, an Old Sidmouthian, for access to
his collection of local material, and to Elizabeth Reed for permission to use items from the
collection of her late husband Gordon, the well-known Sidmouth photographer.

Others who have made pictures available to us are: Marion Baker, Mr and Mrs Ken Clarke,
Noel Collier, Gill Crick, Len and Margery Evis, the *Express & Echo*, John Godfrey of the
Seaton Book Centre, John Goodwin and Sidmouth Cricket Club, Mr and Mrs John Green,
Myrtle Greenway, Paul Hargreaves of the Victoria Steam Laundry, Andrew Harris and
Sidmouth Town Silver Band, Mike Harris, Hilary Hatherleigh and Sidmouth Amateur
Dramatic Society, Clive Hayman, Stuart Hills of Slade's Garage, Dorothy and Larry Jackson,
Mary McKinnon, Maureen Mitchell, John Mortimore, Terence Lee of Potburys, Marion and
Barry Perry, Ted Pinney, Norman Roberts, the *Sidmouth Herald*, which has faithfully chronicled
Sidmouth's history since 1849, Gwen Selway, Alan and Barbara Softly, 'Nobby' Thomas, Steve
Turner of Anstis Butcher's Shop, Roger and Sheila Wills of the Rising Sun at Sidford, Mike
Wood and Sidbury Football Club. Our thanks to them all, especially those who helped us on
our way with cups of tea or coffee.